Writings of Teresa of Ávila

Upper Room Spiritual Classics®

Selected, edited, and introduced by
KEITH BEASLEY-TOPLIFFE

UPPER
ROOM BOOKS®
NASHVILLE

WRITINGS OF TERESA OF ÁVILA
Copyright © 1997 by Upper Room Books
Previously published as *The Soul's Passion for God: Selected Writings of Teresa of Ávila*
All rights reserved.

Upper Room Books' website: books.upperroom.org

Upper Room', Upper Room Books', and design logos are trademarks owned by The Upper Room', Nashville, Tennessee. All rights reserved.

Reprinted from *The Collected Works of St. Teresa of Ávila,* Volume I, translated by Kieran Kavanaugh and Otilio Rodriguez © 1976 by Washington Province of Discalced Carmelites, ICS Publications, 2131 Lincoln Road, NE, Washington, DC 20002 and *The Collected Works of St. Teresa of Ávila,* Volume II, translated by Kieran Kavanaugh and Otilio Rodriguez © 1976 by Washington Province of Discalced Carmelites, ICS Publications, 2131 Lincoln Road, NE, Washington, DC 20002.

Cover design: Tim Green | Faceout Studio
Interior design and typesetting: PerfecType, Nashville, TN

ISBN 978-0-8358-1644-1 (print) | ISBN 978-0-8358-1671-7 (mobi) | ISBN 978-0-8358-1672-4 (epub)

Library of Congress Cataloging-in-Publication Data

Teresa, of Avila, Saint, 1515–1582.
    [Selections. English. 1997]
    The soul's passion for God : selected writings of Teresa of Avila.
        p.   cm.—(Upper Room spiritual classics. Series 1)
    ISBN 0-8358-0828-9 (pbk.)
    Spiritual life—Catholic Church. 2. Meditations. I. Title. II. Series.
BX2179.T3E5 1997
248.4'82-dc21   96-53279
                                                                        CIP

Contents

Introduction

On October 4, 1970, Pope Paul VI proclaimed Teresa of Ávila a Doctor of the Church, that is, an outstanding theological teacher and saint. Although about thirty men had been so designated, Teresa and Catherine of Siena were the first women to receive that title. It was a tribute to both the depth and the popularity of her writings, writings that, during her life, had been censored and impounded by the Inquisition.

Teresa traveled perhaps as far on her spiritual journey as anyone can in this life, finally reaching what she felt was a complete and enduring union with God, which she called a "spiritual marriage." This happened while she was leading a very active life and fighting many chronic diseases, including malaria and arthritis. Fortunately, her confessors ordered her to make time to write about her experiences and her understanding of prayer. She was able to do so with amazing vividness, finding a variety of images to help explain different kinds of prayer.

Teresa's writing repeatedly emphasizes the importance of absolute dependence on God's grace. No human efforts can force God to grant favors to the soul. On the other hand, people do have a responsibility to try to eliminate barriers against grace, habits, and attitudes that tend to keep God at arm's length.

Teresa's World

Spain in the sixteenth century was a nation in turmoil. In 1492, Granada, the last Moorish stronghold, had fallen, and a land where once Jew, Muslim, and Christian had lived more or less peacefully now became exclusively Christian. That same year, Columbus had discovered America. In Teresa's day, the colonization of the New World was proceeding rapidly. Several of Teresa's brothers went there at least temporarily.

Church and state were so intermingled that it was often hard to distinguish between politics and religion. One of the most powerful institutions in Spain was the Inquisition, founded in 1479. Political and economic restrictions had "encouraged" the conversion of many Muslims and Jews. Many of these converts still secretly practiced their original religion, and it was the mission of the Inquisition to find such false Christians and either bring them back into conformity with the church or execute them as heretics. Even though many *conversos* became priests, nuns, even bishops, they were always looked on with some suspicion and lived in danger of being denounced to the Inquisition as secret Jews. Among those so accused in 1485 were Juan Sanchez and his sons Alvaro and Alonso (Teresa's

father), the latter being five years old at the time. Juan con-
fessed his heresy and performed penance. Together with
his sons, he visited each church in Toledo on seven Fridays
while the good Christians spat and threw rocks. Sanchez then
moved his family to Ávila, where he used his second wife's
family name, Cepeda, and bought himself a knighthood, so
that he became Don Juan de Cepeda.

Secret Jews were not the Inquisition's only worry, however.
The Protestant Reformation (which began in 1517) was gain-
ing ground in Germany and France. Any who insisted on the
primacy of grace or on the priesthood of all believers might be
suspect. Even within the Catholic church, there was the danger of "illuminism" or seeking to follow an inner light. Many
claimed special revelations from God, often as God's response
to such acts of devotion as self-starvation or disfigurement. The
Inquisition saw such heresy as the natural result of individual
meditation (sometimes called "mental prayer"). Spoken prayers
(also known as "vocal prayer"), such as the Lord's Prayer, the
Daily Office, or the Mass, were much safer. Many of Teresa's
favorite books on prayer were eventually deemed dangerous
and confiscated. Her own books insist on beginning with
vocal prayer but also on the need to think about what one was
saying, thereby opening the door to mental prayer. Because she
was a woman and a *converso* who was given to mental prayer
and heard voices, it is no wonder the Inquisition kept a close
eye on Teresa.

In Teresa's day, the human mind was described in terms of "faculties." Since Teresa makes much use of this language, it is important to understand it. The mind was seen as having three primary faculties: the will, the intellect, and the memory, all operating more or less independently. Thus Teresa can speak of the will being united to God while the intellect is distracted with many thoughts. When the memory and intellect are quieted and brought back into alignment with the will, this is "recollection." These primary faculties were supported by the five exterior senses as well as the three interior senses: phantasy, which forms internal images based on external or supernatural sensory impression; sense memory, which stores such impressions and images; and imagination, which uses these images to form new images for things not directly experienced. Learning to ignore the constant clamor of these senses is another, more basic sort of recollection.

Teresa's Life

Teresa was born on March 28, 1515, to Alonso de Cepeda and his second wife, Beatriz de Ahumada, the third of their nine children (Alonso also had three children by his first wife). She generally called herself Teresa de Ahumada until she became a nun, when she took the name Teresa of Jesus. Today she is best known by the small town where she was born, Ávila.

Childish fantasies of running away to be martyred by the Moors (a shortcut to heaven) soon gave way to stories of courtly romance between knights in shining armor and beautiful ladies. As she grew into a beautiful young woman, her father caught her becoming overly friendly with her male cousins and bundled her off to a strictly run convent school. Soon she left, due to illness. But she had decided she wanted to be a nun. Her father did not approve.

In 1535, at age twenty, Teresa ran away to the Carmelite Convent of the Incarnation in Ávila and two years later made her final vows as a Carmelite nun. The next year she fell ill again and went home to seek a cure. On the way to visit a famous quack, she stayed with her uncle, who gave her *The Third Spiritual Alphabet* by Francisco de Osuna, a book on mental prayer that opened Teresa's eyes to what prayer could be. The attempted cure, though, nearly killed her. Even when she recovered enough to return to the Incarnation, it was three years before she could walk. Meanwhile, she had shared her new understanding of prayer with her father, who finally had a real conversion to Christianity.

For years, she struggled between prayer and the temptations presented by young men who came to the Incarnation "for spiritual advice." At one time the unworthiness she felt caused her to stop praying (private prayer, that is) for a year and a half. Eventually, a new confessor from the recently formed Jesuit order gave her a copy of Augustine's *Confessions*. When she read of God's grace toward Augustine, who had been a much more accomplished sinner than Teresa, she knew that she really could be forgiven. From that point on (she was then thirty-nine), her spiritual growth was amazing.

It was also bewildering. She began to experience times of prayer in which she was so caught up in a sense of union with God that she appeared to be paralyzed or having a seizure. These are called raptures. When she tried to explain these to her confessors, they decided they were from the devil and ordered her to stop. She could not. Instead she had a growing conviction that God wanted her to reform her order, to restore ideals of poverty and chastity and humility. She was ordered to give up this idea as well, and sent to the home of a rich widow in hope of turning her away from this path.

At this time she was also ordered to write an account of her life and her way of prayer. Soon after she finished, she received permission to found a reformed convent in Ávila, which she named after Saint Joseph. She began with four novices, in August 1562. That winter she wrote *The Way of Perfection* as a manual of prayer for these sisters. The next spring, she switched from shoes to simple sandals, giving her reform the name "Discalced," which means "unshod."

For the next twenty years she founded another fifteen convents, often facing fierce opposition from church and municipal authorities and from the "Calced" Carmelites. All were afraid of possible religious, financial, or sexual scandals that might come from an enclosed convent founded in poverty. Teresa also founded monasteries. One of her first friars was

John of the Cross, perhaps the only one she ever met whose experiences qualified him to understand her spiritual life. She often had to compromise for political reasons, but she held as true to her vision as possible.

In 1572, Teresa experienced the spiritual marriage described above. Five years later, when she was sixty-two, she wrote (again, under orders from her confessor) *The Interior Castle.* Five years after that, on October 4, 1582, she died at the convent she had founded in Alba de Tormes. Forty years later she was declared a saint.

Further Reading

The collected works of Teresa are available in a three-volume paperback edition, translated by Otilio Rodriguez, O.C.D., and Kieran Kavanaugh, O.C.D., published by ICS Publications (Institute of Carmelite Studies). This is the translation used in these selections. There are many biographies of Teresa. An excellent modern one is *Teresa: A Woman* by Victoria Lincoln (State University of New York Press). A shorter and more pious one is *Mother of Carmel* by E. Allison Peers.

Several other Discalced Carmelites have written spiritual classics. ICS Publications has printed recent translations of the works of John of the Cross (1542–91) and Thérèse de Lisieux (1873–97). *The Practice of the Presence of God* by Brother Lawrence (1611–91) is available in several paperback editions.

Key books in Teresa's own reading were *The Third Spiritual Alphabet* by Francisco de Osuna, available from Paulist Press, and the *Confessions* of Saint Augustine, available in many editions.

Note on the Texts

As mentioned above, the ICS translation by Rodriguez and Kavanaugh has been used for these selections, though all have been considerably abridged to keep the length manageable. Teresa wrote rapidly, rarely going back to edit what she had written or even to review what she was writing about when interrupted for a time. Her sentences run on to great length with frequent asides. Occasionally she bursts into prayer. It is truly a conversational style, free-flowing and informal.

Watering the Soul's Garden: The Well

From *The Book of Her Life,* Chapter 11

Teresa began to write The Book of Her Life *in 1562 and completed it in 1565. The centerpiece of the book (Chapters 11–22) is a treatise on prayer. Teresa speaks of different kinds of prayer as different ways of drawing water for the garden of the soul, where virtues grow.*

The beginner must realize that in order to give delight to the Lord he is starting to cultivate a garden on very barren soil, full of abominable weeds. His Majesty pulls up the weeds and plants good seed. Now let us keep in mind that all of this is already done by the time a soul is determined to practice prayer and has begun to make use of it. And with the help of God we must strive like good gardeners to get these plants to grow and take pains to water them so that they don't wither but come to bud and flower and give forth a most pleasant fragrance to provide refreshment for this Lord of ours. Then He will often come to take delight in this garden and find His joy among these virtues.

But let us see now how it must be watered so that we may understand what we have to do, the labor this will cost us, whether the labor is greater than the gain, and for how long it must last. It seems to me the garden can be watered in four ways. You may draw water from a well (which is for us a lot of work). Or you may get it by means of a water wheel and aqueducts in such a way that it is obtained by turning the crank of the water wheel. (I have drawn it this way sometimes—the method involves less work than the other, and you get more water.) Or it may flow from a river or a stream. (The garden is watered much better by this means because the ground is more fully soaked, and there is no need to water so frequently—and much less work for the gardener.) Or the water may be provided by a great deal of rain. (For the Lord waters the garden without any work on our part—and this way is incomparably better than all the others mentioned.)

Now, then, these four ways of drawing water in order to maintain this garden—because without water it will die—are what are important to me and have seemed applicable in explaining the four degrees of prayer in which the Lord in His goodness has sometimes placed my soul.

Beginners in prayer, we can say, are those who draw water from the well. This involves a lot of work on their own part, as I have said. They must tire themselves in trying to recollect their senses. Since they are accustomed to being distracted, this recollection requires much effort. They need to get accustomed to caring nothing at all about seeing or hearing, to practicing the hours of prayer, and thus to solitude and withdrawal—and to thinking on their past life. Although these beginners and the others as well must often reflect upon their past, the extent to which they must do so varies. In the beginning such reflection is even painful, for they do not fully understand whether or not they are repentant of their sins. If they are, they are then determined to serve God earnestly. They must strive to consider the life of Christ—and the intellect grows weary in doing this.

These are the things we can do of ourselves, with the understanding that we do so by the help of God, for without this help as is already known we cannot have so much as a good thought. These things make up the beginning of fetching water from the well, and please God that it may be found. At least we are doing our part, for we are already drawing it out and doing what we can to water these flowers. God is so good that when for reasons His Majesty knows—perhaps for our greater benefit—the well is dry and we, like good gardeners, do what lies in our power, He sustains the garden without water and makes the virtues grow. Here by "water" I am referring to tears and when there are no tears to interior tenderness and feelings of devotion.

But what will he do here who sees that after many days there is nothing but dryness, distaste, vapidness, and very little desire to come to draw water? So little is the desire to do this that if he doesn't recall that doing so serves and gives pleasure to the Lord of the garden, he will abandon everything. It will frequently happen to him that he will even be unable to lift his arms for this work and unable to get a good thought. This discursive work with the intellect is what is meant by fetching water from the well.

But, as I am saying, what will the gardener do here? He will rejoice and be consoled and consider it the greatest favor to be able to work in the garden of so great an Emperor! Since he knows that this pleases the Lord and his intention must be not to please himself but to please the Lord, he gives the Lord much praise. He doesn't fear that the labor is being wasted. He is serving a good Master whose eyes are upon him. He doesn't pay any attention to bad thoughts.

These labors take their toll. Being myself one who endured them for many years, I know that they are extraordinary. It seems to me more courage is necessary for them than for many other labors of this world. But I have seen clearly that God does not leave one, even in this life, without a large reward; because it is certainly true that one of those hours in which the Lord afterward bestowed on me a taste of Himself repaid, it seems to me, all the anguish I suffered in persevering for a long time in prayer.

Watering the Soul's Garden:
The Water Wheel

From *The Book of Her Life,* Chapter 14

Teresa writes of the second method of watering the garden, as the soul becomes recollected and quiet.

It has been explained now how the garden is watered by labor and the use of one's arms, drawing the water up from the well. Let us speak now of the second manner, ordained by the Lord of the garden, for getting water; that is, by turning the crank of a water wheel and by aqueducts, the gardener obtains more water with less labor; and he can rest without having to work constantly. Well, this method applied to what they call the prayer of quiet is what I now want to discuss.

Here the soul begins to be recollected and comes upon something supernatural because in no way can it acquire this prayer through any efforts it may make. True, at one time it seemingly got tired turning the crank, and working with the intellect, and filling the aqueducts. But here the water is higher, and so the labor is much less than that required in pulling it up from the well. I mean that the water is closer because grace is more clearly manifest to the soul.

In this prayer the faculties are gathered within so as to enjoy that satisfaction with greater delight. But they are not lost, nor do they sleep. Only the will is occupied in such a way that, without knowing how it becomes captive; it merely consents to God allowing Him to imprison it as one who well knows how to be the captive of its lover. O Jesus and my Lord! How valuable is Your love to us here! It holds our love so bound that it doesn't allow it the freedom during that time to love anything else but You.

The other two faculties help the will to be capable of enjoying so much good although sometimes it happens that even though the will is united, they are very unhelpful. But then it shouldn't pay any attention to them; rather it should remain in its joy and quietude. Because if the will desires to gather in these faculties, they both get lost. They are like doves that are dissatisfied with the food the owner of the dovecote gives them without their having to work. They go to look for food elsewhere, but they find it so scarce that they return. And thus these faculties go away and then come back to see if the will might give them what it enjoys. If the Lord desires to throw them some food, they stop; and if not, they return to their search. And they must think they are benefiting the will; and sometimes in desiring the memory or imagination to represent to the will what they're enjoying, they do the will harm.

All this that takes place here brings with it the greatest consolation and with so little labor that prayer does not tire one, even though it lasts for a long while. The intellect's work here is very slow paced, and it obtains a lot more water than it pulled out of the well. The tears God gives are now accompanied by joy; however, although they are experienced, there is no striving for them.

This water of great blessings and favors that the Lord gives here makes the virtues grow incomparably better than in the previous degree of prayer, for the soul is now ascending above its misery and receiving a little knowledge of the delights of glory. This water I believe makes the virtues grow better and also brings the soul much closer to the true Virtue, which is God, from whence come all the virtues. His Majesty is beginning to communicate Himself to this soul, and He wants it to experience how He is doing so.

In arriving here it begins soon to lose its craving for earthly things—and little wonder! It sees clearly that one moment of the enjoyment of glory cannot be experienced here below, neither are there riches, or sovereignties, or honors, or delights that are able to provide a brief moment of that happiness, for it is a true happiness that, it is seen, satisfies us. In earthly things it would seem to me a marvel were we ever to understand just where we can find this satisfaction, for there is never lacking in these earthly things both the "yes" and the "no." During the time of this prayer, everything is "yes." The "no" comes afterward upon seeing that the delight is ended and that one cannot recover it—nor does one know how. Were someone to crush himself with penances and prayer and all the rest, it would profit him little if the Lord did not desire to give this delight. God in His greatness desires that this soul understand that He is so close it no longer needs to send Him messengers but can speak with Him itself and not by shouting since He is so near that when it merely moves its lips, He understands it.

Let us now return to our garden and see how these trees are beginning to bud so as to blossom and afterward give fruit— and also the flowers and carnations so as to give forth their fragrance. This comparison has its charm for me because often in my beginnings it was a great delight for me to consider my soul as a garden and reflect that the Lord was taking His walk in it. I begged Him to increase the fragrance of the little flowers of virtue that were beginning to bloom, so it seemed, and that they might give Him glory and He might sustain them since I desired nothing for myself—and that He might cut the ones He wanted, for I already knew that better ones would flower. I say "cut" because there are times when the soul has no thought of this garden. Everything seems to be dry, and it seems there is not going to be any water to sustain it nor does it appear that there has ever been in the soul anything of virtue. It undergoes much tribulation because the Lord desires that it seem to the poor gardener that everything acquired in watering and keeping the garden up is being lost. This dryness amounts to an authentic weeding and pulling up of the remaining bad growth by its roots, no matter how small it may be. By knowing that there is no diligence that suffices if God takes away the water of grace and by placing little value on the nothing that we are, and even less than nothing, the soul gains much humility. The flowers begin to grow again.

Watering the Soul's Garden:
The Spring

From *The Book of Her Life,* Chapter 16

Teresa writes about the prayer of quiet as the third "water."

Let us come now to speak of the third water by which this garden is irrigated, that is, the water flowing from a river or spring. By this means the garden is irrigated with much less labor, although some labor is required to direct the flow of the water. The Lord so desires to help the gardener here that He Himself becomes practically the gardener and the one who does everything.

This prayer is a sleep of the faculties: the faculties neither fail entirely to function nor understand how they function. The consolation, the sweetness, and the delight are incomparably greater than that experienced in the previous prayer. The water of grace rises up to the throat of this soul since it can no longer move forward; nor does it know how; nor can it move backward. It would desire to enjoy the greatest glory. It is like a person who already has the candle in his hand and for whom little time is left before dying the death he desires: he is rejoicing in that agony with the greatest delight describable. This experience doesn't seem to me to be anything else than an almost complete death to all earthly things and an enjoyment of God.

I don't know any other terms for describing it or how to explain it. Nor does the soul then know what to do because it doesn't know whether to speak or to be silent, whether to laugh or to weep. This prayer is a glorious foolishness, a heavenly madness where the true wisdom is learned; and it is for the soul a most delightful way of enjoying.

In fact five or even six years ago the Lord often gave me this prayer in abundance, and I didn't understand it; nor did I know how to speak of it. I did understand clearly that it was not a complete union of all the faculties and that this type of prayer was more excellent than the previous one. But I confess that I couldn't discern or understand where the difference lay. The Lord today after Communion granted me this prayer; and interrupting my thanksgiving, He put before me these comparisons, taught me the manner of explaining it, and what the soul must do here. For the truth of the matter is that the faculties are almost totally united with God but not so absorbed as not to function. I am extremely pleased that I now understand it. Blessed be the Lord who so favored me!

The faculties have only the ability to be occupied completely with God. It doesn't seem that any one of them dares to move, nor can we make them stir unless we strain to distract ourselves; but even then I don't think we could do so entirely. One utters many words here in praise of God without thinking them up, unless it is the Lord who thinks them up; at least the intellect is worth nothing here. The soul would desire to cry out praises, and it is beside itself—a delightful disquiet. Now the flowers are blossoming; they are beginning to spread their fragrance. The soul would desire here that everyone could see and understand its glory so as to praise God and that they would all help it to praise Him and share in its joy since it cannot bear so much joy. I think it is like what is said in the Gospels about the woman that wanted to call or did call in her neighbors.

Oh, help me God! What is the soul like when it is in this state! It would want to be all tongues so as to praise the Lord. It speaks folly in a thousand holy ways, ever trying to find means of pleasing the one who thus possesses it. I know a person who though not a poet suddenly composed some deeply felt verses well expressing her pain. They were not composed by the use of her intellect; rather, in order that she enjoy the glory so delightful a distress gave to her, she complained of it in this way to God.

Well, it doesn't seem to me that I have exaggerated. Nothing can compare with the delight the Lord desires a soul to enjoy in this exile. May You be blessed forever, Lord! May all things praise You forever! Since while I write this I am not freed from such holy, heavenly madness coming from Your goodness and mercy—for You grant this favor without any merits on my part at all—either desire, my King, I beseech You, that all to whom I speak become mad from Your love, or do not permit that I speak to anyone! Either ordain, Lord, that I no longer pay attention to anything in the world, or take me out of it! This soul would now want to see itself free—eating kills it; sleeping distresses it. It observes that its lifetime is passing in pleasure and that nothing other than You can give it pleasure any longer; for since it desires to live no longer in itself but in You, it seems that its life is unnatural.

O true Lord and my Glory! How delicate and extremely heavy a cross You have prepared for those who reach this state! "Delicate" because it is pleasing; "heavy" because there come times when there is no capacity to bear it; and yet the soul would never want to be freed from it unless it were for the sake of being with You. When it recalls that it hasn't served You in anything and that by living it can serve You, it would want to carry a much heavier cross and never die until the end of the world. It finds no rest in anything except in doing You some small service. It doesn't know what it wants, but it well understands that it wants nothing other than You.

Watering the Soul's Garden: Rain

From *The Book of Her Life*, Chapter 18

Teresa describes the prayer of union and its accompanying raptures and ecstasy as the fourth "water," when the gardener does nothing but enjoy the rain falling from on high.

May the Lord teach me the words necessary for explaining something about the fourth water. Clearly His favor is necessary, even more so than for what was explained previously. In the previous prayer, since the soul was conscious of the world, it did not feel that it was totally dead—for we can speak of this last prayer in such a way. But, as I said, the soul has its senses by which it feels its solitude and understands that it is in the world; and it uses exterior things to make known what it feels, even though this may be through signs.

In all the prayer and modes of prayer that were explained, the gardener does some work, even though in these latter modes the work is accompanied by so much glory and consolation for the soul that it would never want to abandon this prayer. As a result, the prayer is not experienced as work but as glory. In this fourth water the soul isn't in possession of its

senses, but it rejoices without understanding what it is rejoicing in. It understands that it is enjoying a good in which are
gathered together all goods, but this good is incomprehensible.
All the senses are occupied in this joy in such a way that none
is free to be taken up with any other exterior or interior thing.

In the previous degrees, the senses are given freedom to
show some signs of the great joy they feel. Here in this fourth
water the soul rejoices incomparably more; but it can show
much less since no power remains in the body, nor does the
soul have any power to communicate its joy. And if it were
able, then this wouldn't be union.

How this prayer they call union comes about and what it
is, I don't know how to explain. Neither do I understand what
the mind is; nor do I know how it differs from the soul or the
spirit. It all seems to be the same thing to me, although the
soul sometimes goes forth from itself. The way this happens is
comparable to what happens when a fire is burning and flam-
ing, and it sometimes becomes a forceful blaze. The flame then
shoots very high above the fire, but the flame is not by that
reason something different from the fire but the same flame
that is in the fire.

What I'm attempting to explain is what the soul feels when
it is in this divine union. What union is we already know since
it means that two separate things become one. O my Lord,
how good You are! May You be blessed forever! May all things

praise You, my God, for You have so loved us that we can truthfully speak of this communication which You engage in with souls even in our exile! And even in the case of those who are good, this still shows great generosity and magnanimity. In fact, it is Your communication, my Lord; and You give it in the manner of who You are.

Well now, let us speak of this heavenly water that in its abundance soaks and saturates this entire garden: if the Lord were always to give it when there is need, the gardener would evidently have it easy. And if there were no winter and the weather were always mild, there would be no lack of flowers and fruit. It is obvious how delighted the gardener would be. But this is impossible while we are living on this earth. A person must always take care so that when one kind of water is lacking he might strive for the other. This water from heaven often comes when the gardener is least expecting it. True, in the beginning it almost always occurs after a long period of mental prayer. The Lord comes to take this tiny bird from one degree to another and to place it in the nest so that it may have repose. Since He has seen it fly about for a long time, striving with the intellect and the will and all its strength to see God and please Him, He desires to reward it even in this life. And what a tremendous reward; one moment is enough to repay all the trials that can be suffered in life!

While the soul is seeking God in this way, it feels with the most marvelous and gentlest delight that everything is almost fading away through a kind of swoon in which breathing and all the bodily energies gradually fail. This experience comes about in such a way that one cannot even stir the hands without a lot of effort. The eyes close without one's wanting them to close; or if a person keeps them open, he sees hardly anything. He hears but doesn't understand what he hears. Thus he receives no benefit from the senses—unless it be that they do not take away his pleasure since doing so would cause harm. In vain does he try to speak because he doesn't succeed in forming a word, nor if he does succeed is there the strength left to be able to pronounce it. All the external energy is lost, and that of the soul is increased so that it might better enjoy its glory. The exterior delight that is felt is great and very distinct.

This prayer causes no harm, no matter how long it lasts. At least it never caused me any nor do I recall the Lord ever having granted me this favor that I didn't feel much better afterward no matter how ill I had been before. But what illness can produce so wonderful a blessing? The external effects are so apparent that one cannot doubt that a great event has taken place; these external powers are taken away with such delight in order to leave greater ones.

After having received Communion and been in this very prayer I'm writing about, I was thinking when I wanted to write something on it of what the soul did during that time. The Lord spoke these words to me: "It detaches itself from everything, daughter, so as to abide more in me. It is no longer the soul that lives but I. Since it cannot comprehend what it understands, there is an understanding by not understanding."

In this prayer all the faculties fail and they are so suspended that in no way, as I said, does one think they are working. If a person is reflecting upon some scriptural event, it becomes as lost to the memory as it would be if there had never been any thought of it. If the person reads, there is no remembrance of what he read; nor is there any remembrance if he prays vocally. Thus this bothersome little moth, which is the memory, gets its wings burnt here; it can no longer move. The will is fully occupied in loving, but it doesn't understand how it loves. The intellect, if it understands, doesn't understand how it understands.

The Prayer the Lord Gives You

From *The Way of Perfection*, Chapter 17

Teresa wrote The Way of Perfection *in 1565 as a manual for the nuns of the first convent she established, St. Joseph's in Ávila. Here she urges the sisters to accept the individual paths of prayer by which God leads them.*

It seems I am already dealing with prayer. But something still remains to be said that is very important because it pertains to humility and is necessary in this house where the main occupation is prayer. And, as I have said, it is only right that you should try to understand how to train yourselves a great deal in humility. Yes, it is true, God can make you a contemplative—through His goodness and mercy; but, in my opinion, one should always take the lowest place, for this is what the Lord told us to do and taught us in deed. Prepare yourself so that God may lead you along this path if He so desires. When He doesn't, you can practice humility, which is to consider yourself lucky to serve the servants of the Lord and praise His Majesty because He brought you among them and drew you away from the devils in hell.

It is important to understand that God doesn't lead all by one path, and perhaps the one who thinks she is walking along a very lowly path is in fact higher in the eyes of the Lord. And it would be very distressing for the one who isn't a contemplative if she didn't understand the truth that to be a contemplative is a gift from God; and since being one isn't necessary for salvation, nor does God demand this, she shouldn't think anyone will demand it of her.

I spent fourteen years never being able to practice meditation without reading. There will be many persons of this sort, and others who will be unable to meditate even with the reading but able only to pray vocally, and in this vocal prayer they will spend most of their time. There are minds so active they cannot dwell on one thing but are always restless, and to such an extreme that if they want to pause to think of God, a thousand absurdities, scruples, and doubts come to mind.

I know an elderly person who lives a good life, is penitential and an excellent servant of God, who has spent many hours for many years in vocal prayer, but in mental prayer she's helpless; the most she can do is go slowly in reciting the vocal prayers. There are a number of other persons of this kind. If humility is present I don't believe they will be any the worse off in the end but will be very much the equals of those who receive many delights; and in a way they will be more secure, for we do not know if the delights are from God or from the devil.

Those who do not receive these delights walk with humility, suspecting that this lack is their own fault, always concerned about making progress. They don't see anyone shed a tear without thinking that if they themselves don't shed any they are very far behind in the service of God. In humility, mortification, detachment, and the other virtues there is always greater security. There is nothing to fear; don't be afraid that you will fail to reach the perfection of those who are very contemplative.

Saint Martha was a saint, even though they do not say she was contemplative. Well now, what more do you want than to be able to resemble this blessed woman who merited so often to have Christ our Lord in her home, give Him food, serve Him and eat at table with Him? If she had been enraptured like the Magdalene, there wouldn't have been anyone to give food to the divine Guest. Well, think of this congregation as the home of Saint Martha and that there must be people for every task. And those who are led by the active life shouldn't complain about those who are very much absorbed in contemplation, for these active ones know that the Lord will defend the contemplatives, even though these latter are silent since for the most part contemplation makes one forgetful of self and of all things.

Let them recall that it is necessary for someone to prepare His meal and let them consider themselves lucky to serve with Martha. Let them consider how true humility consists very much in great readiness to be content with whatever the Lord may want to do with them and in always finding oneself unworthy to be called His servant. If contemplating, practicing mental and vocal prayer, taking care of the sick, helping with household chores, and working even at the lowliest tasks are all ways of serving the Guest who comes to be with us and eat and recreate, what difference does it make whether we serve in the one way or the other?

I don't say that we shouldn't try; on the contrary, we should try everything. What I am saying is that this is not a matter of your choosing but of the Lord's. If after many years He should give to each a certain task, it would be a nice kind of humility for you to want to choose for yourselves. Leave it up to the Lord of the house; He is wise, He is mighty, He understands what is suitable for you and what is suitable for Him as well. Be sure that if you do what lies in your power, preparing yourselves for contemplation with the perfection mentioned, and that if He doesn't give it to you (and I believe He will give it if detachment and humility are truly present), He will save this gift for you so as to grant it to you all at once in heaven. And, as I have said before, He wants to lead you as though you were strong, giving you the cross here below, something that His Majesty always had. What better friendship than that He desire for you what He desired for Himself?

And it could be that you would not have received so great an award in contemplation.

O wonderful gain, not to want to gain from following our own judgment lest we suffer any loss! God, in fact, never permits any loss to come to a person truly mortified save for greater gain.

The Lord's Prayer:
Your Kingdom Come

From *The Way of Perfection,* Chapter 20

The last sixteen chapters of The Way of Perfection *are a commentary on the Lord's Prayer (referred to here as the "Our Father"). Teresa insists that vocal prayer must be accompanied by thought about what is being said and so leads inevitably to mental prayer. Here she comments on "Your kingdom come."*

It is good, daughters, that you understand what you are asking for in the Our Father so that if the Eternal Father should offer it to you, you will not scoff at it. And consider very carefully whether what you ask for is good for you; if it isn't, don't ask for it, but ask His Majesty to give you light. For we are blind and feel loathing for the food that will give us life; we want the food that will bring us death. And what a death! So dangerous and so everlasting!

Well, Jesus says that we may recite these words in which we ask for a kingdom like His to come within us: "Hallowed be Your name, Your kingdom come within us."

Now behold, daughters, how great the wisdom of our Master is. I am reflecting here on what we are asking for when we ask for this kingdom, and it is good that we understand our request. But since His Majesty saw that we could neither hallow nor praise, nor extol, nor glorify this holy name of the Eternal Father in a fitting way because of the tiny amount we ourselves are capable of doing, He provided for us by giving us here on earth His kingdom. That is why Jesus put these two petitions next to each other. I want to tell you here, daughters, what I understand so that we may know what we are asking for and the importance of our begging persistently for it, and do as much as we can so as to please the One who is to give it to us. If I do not satisfy you, you can think up other reflections yourselves. Our Master will allow us to make these reflections provided that we submit in all things to what the Church holds, as I do.

Now, then, the great good that it seems to me there will be in the kingdom of heaven, among many other blessings, is that one will no longer take any account of earthly things, but have a calmness and glory within, rejoice in the fact that all are rejoicing, experience perpetual peace and a wonderful inner satisfaction that comes from seeing that everyone hallows and praises the Lord and blesses His name and that no one offends Him. Everyone loves Him there, and the soul itself doesn't think about anything else than loving Him; nor can it cease loving Him, because it knows Him. And would that we could love Him in this way here below, even though we may not be able to do so with such perfection or stability. But if we knew Him we would love in a way very different from that in which we do love Him.

It seems I'm saying that we would have to be angels in order to make this petition and recite well our vocal prayers. Our divine Master would truly desire this since He asks us to make so lofty a petition, and certainly He doesn't tell us to ask for impossible things. The above would be possible, through the favor of God, for a soul placed in this exile, but not with the perfection of those who have gone forth from this prison; for we are at sea and journeying along this way. But there are times when, tired from our travels, we experience that the Lord calms our faculties and quiets the soul. As though by signs, He gives us a clear foretaste of what will be given to those He brings to His kingdom. And to those to whom He gives here below the kingdom we ask for, He gives pledges so that through these they may have great hope of going to enjoy perpetually what here on earth is given only in sips.

If you wouldn't say that I'm treating of contemplation, this petition would provide a good opportunity for speaking a little about the beginning of pure contemplation; those who experience this prayer call it the prayer of quiet. But since, as I say, I'm dealing with vocal prayer, it may seem to anyone who doesn't know about the matter that vocal prayer doesn't go with contemplation; but I know that it does. Pardon me, but I want to say this: I know there are many persons who while praying vocally are raised by God to sublime contemplation without their striving for anything or understanding how. It's because of this that I insist so much, daughters, upon your reciting vocal prayer well. I know a person who was never able to pray any way but vocally, and though she was tied to this form of prayer she experienced everything else. And if she didn't recite vocal prayer her mind wandered so much that she couldn't bear it. Would that our mental prayer were as good! She spent several hours reciting a certain number of Our Fathers, in memory of the times our Lord shed His blood, as well as a few other vocal prayers. Once she came to me very afflicted because she didn't know how to practice mental prayer nor could she contemplate; she could only pray vocally. I asked her how she was praying, and I saw that though she was tied to the Our Father she experienced pure contemplation and that the Lord was raising her up and joining her with Himself in union. And from her deeds it seemed truly that she was receiving such great favors, for she was living a very good life. So I praised the Lord and envied her for her vocal prayer.

The Lord's Prayer: Our Daily Bread

From *The Way of Perfection,* Chapter 34

Teresa writes about how to receive Communion as "our bread."

In no matter how many ways the soul may desire to eat, it will find delight and consolation in the most Blessed Sacrament. There is no need or trial or persecution that is not easy to suffer if we begin to enjoy the delight and consolation of this sacred bread.

Do you think this heavenly food fails to provide sustenance, even for these bodies, that it is not a great medicine even for bodily ills? I know that it is. I know a person with serious illnesses, who often experiences great pain, who through this bread had them taken away as though by gesture of the hand and was made completely well. And because the wonders this most sacred bread effects in those who worthily receive it are well known, I will not mention many that could be mentioned regarding this person I've spoken of. But the Lord had given her such living faith that when she heard some persons saying they would have liked to have lived at the time Christ our God walked in the world, she used to laugh to herself. She wondered what more they wanted since in the most Blessed Sacrament they had Him just as truly present as He was then.

But I know that for many years, when she received Communion, this person, though she was not very perfect, strove to strengthen her faith so that in receiving her Lord it was as if, with her bodily eyes, she saw Him enter her house. Since she believed that this Lord truly entered her poor home, she freed herself from all exterior things when it was possible and entered to be with Him. She strove to recollect the senses so that all of them would take notice of so great a good, I mean that they would not impede the soul from recognizing it. She considered she was at His feet and wept with the Magdalene, no more nor less than if she were seeing Him with her bodily eyes in the house of the Pharisee. And even though she didn't feel devotion, faith told her that He was indeed there.

If we don't want to be fools and blind the intellect there's no reason for doubt. Receiving Communion is not like picturing with the imagination, as when we reflect upon the Lord on the cross or in other episodes of the Passion, when we picture within ourselves how things happened to Him in the past. In Communion the event is happening now, and it is entirely true. There's no reason to go looking for Him in some other place farther away. Now, then, if when He went about in the world the mere touch of His robes cured the sick, why doubt, if we have faith, that miracles will be worked while He is within us and that He will give what we ask of Him, since He is in our house? His Majesty is not accustomed to paying poorly for His lodging if the hospitality is good.

Oh, how we fail to know what we are asking for; and how His wisdom provided in a better way! He reveals Himself to those who He sees will benefit by His presence. Even though they fail to see Him with their bodily eyes, He has many methods of showing Himself to the soul, through great interior feelings and through other different ways. Be with Him willingly; don't lose so good an occasion for conversing with Him as is the hour after having received Communion. If obedience should command something, Sisters, strive to leave your soul with the Lord. If you immediately turn your thoughts to other things, if you pay no attention and take no account of the fact that He is within you, how will He be able to reveal Himself to you? This, then, is a good time for our Master to teach us, and for us to listen to Him, kiss His feet because He wanted to teach us, and beg Him not to leave.

But after having received the Lord, since you have the Person Himself present, strive to close the eyes of the body and open those of the soul and look into your own heart. For I tell you, and tell you again, and would like to tell you many times that you should acquire the habit of doing this every time you receive Communion and strive to have such a conscience that you will be allowed to enjoy this blessing frequently. Though He comes disguised, the disguise as I have said, does not prevent Him from being recognized in many ways, in conformity with the desire we have to see Him. And you can desire to see Him so much that He will reveal Himself to you entirely.

On the other hand, if we pay no attention to Him but after receiving Him leave Him and go seeking after other base things, what is there for Him to do? Must He force us to see Him, since He wants to reveal Himself to us? No, for they didn't treat Him so well when He let Himself be seen openly by all and told them clearly who He was; very few were those who believed Him. So His Majesty is being merciful enough to all of us who love Him, by letting us know that it is He who is present in the most Blessed Sacrament. He doesn't want to show Himself openly, communicate His grandeurs, and give His treasures except to those who He knows desire Him greatly; these are His true friends. I tell you that whoever is not His true friend and does not draw near to receive Him as such, by doing what lies in her power, will never trouble Him with requests that He reveal Himself. Such a person will hardly have fulfilled what the Church requires when she will leave and quickly forget what took place. Thus, such a person hurries on as soon she can to other business affairs, occupations, and worldly impediments so that the Lord of the house may not occupy it.

The Lord's Prayer: Forgive Us Our Debts

From *The Way of Perfection,* Chapter 36

Teresa continues her commentary on the Lord's Prayer with "forgive us our debts."

Since our good Master saw that with this heavenly bread everything is easy for us, save through our own fault, and that we can carry out very well what we have said about the Father's will being done in us, He now tells the Father to forgive us our debts since we ourselves forgive. Thus, He says, going on with the prayer He teaches us, "And forgive us, Lord, our debts as we forgive our debtors."

Let us observe, Sisters, that He doesn't say "as we will forgive." We can thereby understand that whoever asks for a gift as great as the one last mentioned and whoever has already surrendered his will to God's will should have already forgiven. So, He says, "as we forgive."

You see here why the saints were pleased with the wrongs and persecutions they suffered; they then had something to offer the Lord when they prayed to Him. What will someone as poor as I do, who has had so little to pardon and so much to be pardoned for?

This is a matter, Sisters, that we should reflect upon very much: that something so serious and important, as that our Lord forgive us our faults, which deserve eternal fire, be done by means of something so lowly as our forgiving others. And I have so little opportunity to offer even this lowly thing, that the Lord has to pardon me for nothing.

But, my Lord, are there some persons in my company who have not understood this? If there are, I beg them in Your name to remember this and pay no attention to the little things they call wrongs. It seems that, like children, we are making houses out of straw with these ceremonious little rules of etiquette. Oh, God help me, Sisters, if we knew what honor is and what losing honor consists in! Now I am not speaking of ourselves, for it would be quite bad for us not to have understood this yet, but of myself at the time when I prized honor without understanding what it was. I was following the crowd. Oh, by how many things was I offended! I am ashamed now.

Oh, for the love of God, Sisters, how we get lost on the road because we start out wrong from the beginning. Please God no soul will be lost because it keeps these miserable little rules of etiquette without understanding what honor consists in. And then we shall reach the point of thinking that we have done a great deal if we pardon one of these little things that was neither an offense, nor an injury, nor anything. Like someone who has accomplished something, we shall think that the Lord pardons us because we have pardoned others. Help us understand, my God, that we do not know ourselves and that we come to You with empty hands; and pardon us through Your mercy.

But yet, how the Lord must esteem this love we have for one another! Indeed, Jesus could have put other virtues first and said: forgive us, Lord, because we do a great deal of penance or because we pray much and fast or because we have left all for You and love You very much. He didn't say forgive us because we would give up our lives for You, or, as I say, because of other possible things. But He said only, "forgive us because we forgive." Perhaps He said the prayer and offered it on our behalf because He knows we are so fond of this miserable honor and that to be forgiving is a virtue difficult for us to attain by ourselves but most pleasing to His Father.

Well, consider carefully, Sisters, that He says, "as we forgive," as though it were something already being done, as I have mentioned. And pay very close attention, for when among the favors God grants in the prayer of perfect contemplation that I mentioned there doesn't arise in the soul a very resolute desire to pardon any injury however grave it may be and to pardon it in deed when the occasion arises, do not trust much in that soul's prayer. And I don't refer to these nothings that they call injuries. For the soul God brings to Himself in so sublime a contemplation is not touched by these wrongs nor does it care at all whether it is esteemed or not. I didn't say this well, "nor does it care at all," for it is much more afflicted by honor than by dishonor and by a lot of ease and rest than by trials. For when truly the Lord has given His kingdom here below, the soul no longer desires honor in this world.

Now then, Sisters, realize that since these contemplatives already know what everything is worth, they are not long delayed by a passing thing. If at first a great affront or trial causes pain, their reason comes to their rescue, before the pain is fully felt, with another consideration as if to raise the banner and almost annihilate the pain by means of joy. This joy comes from their seeing that the Lord has placed in their hands something by which they will gain more graces and perpetual favors from His Majesty than they would in ten years through trials they might wish to undertake on their own.

Self-esteem is far removed from these persons. They like others to know about their sins and like to tell about them when they see themselves esteemed. The same is true in matters concerning their lineage. They already know that in the kingdom without end they will have nothing to gain from this. If they should happen to be pleased to be of good descent, it's when this would be necessary in order to serve God. When it isn't, it grieves them to be taken for more than what they are, and without any grief at all but gladly they disillusion others.

So it is with those to whom God grants the grace of this humility and great love for Himself. In what amounts to His greater service, they are already so forgetful of self that they can't even believe that others feel some things and consider them an affront.

I cannot believe that a person who comes so close to Mercy itself, where he realizes what he is and the great deal God has pardoned him of, would fail to pardon his offender immediately, in complete ease, and with a readiness to remain on very good terms with him. Such a person is mindful of the gift and favor granted by God, by which he saw signs of great love; and he rejoices that an opportunity is offered whereby he can show the Lord some love. Since Jesus knows this well, He says resolutely to His holy Father that "we pardon our debtors."

The Lord's Prayer: Temptations

From *The Way of Perfection*, Chapter 39

Teresa writes about some of the temptations that may come to those who pray.

Now be also on your guard, daughters, against some types of humility given by the devil in which great disquiet is felt about the gravity of our sins. This disturbance can afflict in many ways even to the point of making one give up receiving Communion and practicing private prayer. These things are given up because the devil makes one feel unworthy. And when such persons approach the Blessed Sacrament, the time they used to spend in receiving favors is now spent in wondering whether or not they are well prepared. The situation gets so bad that the soul thinks God has abandoned it because of what it is; it almost doubts His mercy. Everything it deals with seems dangerous, and what it uses, however good, seems fruitless. It feels such distrust of itself that it folds its arms and remains idle; what is good in others seems evil when the soul sees it within its own self.

Consider carefully, daughters, the matter I'm going to speak to you about, for sometimes it will be through humility and virtue that you hold yourselves to be so wretched, and at other times it will be a gross temptation. I know of this because I have gone through it. Humility does not disturb or disquiet or agitate, however great it may be; it comes with peace, delight, and calm. Even though a person upon seeing himself so wretched understands clearly that he merits to be in hell, suffers affliction, thinks everyone should in justice abhor him, and almost doesn't dare ask for mercy, his pain, if the humility is genuine, comes with a sweetness in itself and a satisfaction that he wouldn't want to be without. The pain of genuine humility doesn't agitate or afflict the soul; rather, this humility expands it and enables it to serve God more. The other type of pain disturbs everything, agitates everything, afflicts the entire soul, and is very painful. I think the devil's aim is to make us think we are humble and, in turn, if possible, make us lose confidence in God.

When you find yourselves in this condition, stop thinking about your misery, insofar as possible, and turn your thoughts to the mercy of God, to how He loves us and suffered for us. And if you are undergoing a temptation, you will not even be able to do this, for the devil will not let you quiet your mind or concentrate on anything unless so as to tire you all the more. It will be enough if you recognize that this is a temptation.

The devil sets up another dangerous temptation: self-assurance in the thought that we will in no way return to our past faults and worldly pleasures: "for now I have understood the world and know that all things come to an end and that the things of God give me greater delight." If this self-assurance is present in beginners, it is very dangerous because with it a person doesn't take care against entering once more into the occasions of sin, and he falls flat; please God the relapse will not bring about something much worse. For since the devil sees that he is dealing with a soul that can do him harm and bring profit to others, he uses all his power so that it might not rise.

Thus, however many delights and pledges of love the Lord gives you, never proceed with such self-assurance that you stop fearing lest you fall again; and be on guard against the occasions of sin.

Strive, without hiding anything, to discuss these favors and consolations with someone who will enlighten you. And take care about this: however sublime the contemplation, let your prayer always begin and end with self-knowledge. And if the favor is from God, even though you may not want to follow the advice, you will still follow it most of the time because God's favor brings humility and always leaves greater light that we may understand the little that we are.

Thus, Eternal Father, what can we do but have recourse to You and pray that these enemies of ours not lead us into temptation? Let public enemies come, for by Your favor we will be more easily freed. But these other treacheries; who will understand them, my God? We always need to pray to You for a remedy. Instruct us, Lord, so that we may understand ourselves and be secure. You already know that few take the path; but if they have to travel it with so many fears, many fewer will take it.

Unless it is very much due to their own fault, souls who practice prayer walk so much more securely than those who take another road. They are like those in the stands watching the bull in comparison with one who is right in front of its horns. I have heard this comparison, and it seems to me true to the letter.

Do not fear, Sisters, to travel these paths, for in prayer there are many. Some souls profit by one path, and others by another, as I have said. Prayer is a safe road; you will be more quickly freed from temptation when close to the Lord than when far. Beseech Him and ask Him to deliver you from evil as you do so often each day in the Our Father.

The Soul as a Crystal Castle

From *The Interior Castle, First Dwelling Places,* Chapter 1

In 1577, Teresa wrote her most complete account of the spiritual life, The Interior Castle. *In this passage she explains the image of the castle and the beginnings of prayer.*

Today while beseeching our Lord to speak for me, there came to my mind what I shall now speak about. It is that we consider our soul to be like a castle made entirely out of a diamond or of very clear crystal, in which there are many rooms, just as in heaven there are many dwelling places. For in reflecting upon it carefully, Sisters, we realize that the soul of the just person is nothing else but a paradise where the Lord says He finds His delight. So then, what do you think that abode will be like where a King so powerful, so wise, so pure, so full of all good things takes His delight? I don't find anything comparable to the magnificent beauty of a soul and its marvelous capacity.

It is a shame and unfortunate that through our own fault we don't understand ourselves or know who we are. Wouldn't it show great ignorance, my daughters, if someone when asked who he was didn't know, and didn't know his father or mother or from what country he came? Well now, if this would be so extremely stupid, we are incomparably more so when we do not strive to know who we are, but limit ourselves to considering only roughly these bodies. Because we have heard and because faith tells us so, we know we have souls. But we seldom consider the precious things that can be found in this soul, or who dwells within it, or its high value. Consequently, little effort is made to preserve its beauty. All our attention is taken up with the plainness of the diamond's setting or the outer wall of the castle; that is, with these bodies of ours.

Well, let us consider that this castle has, as I said, many dwelling places: some up above, others down below, others to the sides; and in the center and middle is the main dwelling place where the very secret exchanges between God and the soul take place.

But you must understand that there is a great difference in the ways one may be inside the castle. For there are many souls who are in the outer courtyard—which is where the guards stay—and don't care at all about entering the castle, nor do they know what lies within that most precious place, nor who is within, nor even how many rooms it has. You have already heard in some books on prayer that the soul is advised to enter within itself; well, that's the very thing I'm advising.

Not long ago a very learned man told me that souls who do not practice prayer are like people with paralyzed or crippled bodies; even though they have hands and feet they cannot give orders to these hands and feet. Thus there are souls so ill and so accustomed to being involved in external matters that there is no remedy, nor does it seem they can enter within themselves. They are now so used to dealing always with the insects and vermin that are in the wall surrounding the castle that they have become almost like them. And though they have so rich a nature and the power to converse with none other than God, there is no remedy.

Insofar as I can understand the door of entry to this castle is prayer and reflection. I don't mean to refer to mental more than vocal prayer, for since vocal prayer is prayer it must be accompanied by reflection. A prayer in which a person is not aware of whom he is speaking to, what he is asking, who it is who is asking and of whom, I do not call prayer however much the lips move. Sometimes it will be so without this reflection provided that the soul has these reflections at other times. Nonetheless, anyone who has the habit of speaking before God's majesty as though he were speaking to a slave, without being careful to see how he is speaking, but saying whatever comes to his head and whatever he has learned from saying at other times, in my opinion is not praying. Please God, may no Christian pray in this way.

Well now, we are not speaking to these crippled souls. But we are speaking to other souls that, in the end, enter the castle. For even though they are very involved in the world, they have good desires and sometimes, though only once in a while, they entrust themselves to our Lord and reflect on who they are, although in a rather hurried fashion. During the period of a month they will sometimes pray, but their minds are then filled with business matters which ordinarily occupy them. They are so attached to these things that where their treasure lies their heart goes also. Sometimes they do put all these things aside, and the self-knowledge and awareness that they are not proceeding correctly in order to get to the door is important. Finally, they enter the first, lower rooms. But so many reptiles get in with them that they are prevented from seeing the beauty of the castle and from calming down; they have done quite a bit just by having entered.

Consolations in Prayer

From *The Interior Castle, Fourth Dwelling Places,*
Chapter 1

The second dwelling places saw the beginning of disciplined prayer. In the third dwelling places, discursive meditation was the primary way of prayer (like the bucket and well of the first "water" in The Book of Her Life. *In the fourth dwelling places, supernatural prayer begins. That is, God begins to take over. First, though, Teresa writes about the consolations that can come from our own efforts in prayer.*

Well now, in speaking about the difference in prayer between consolations and spiritual delights, the term "consolations," I think, can be given to those experiences we ourselves acquire through our own meditation and petitions to the Lord, those that proceed from our own nature—although God in the end does have a hand in them; for it must be understood, in whatever I say, that without Him we can do nothing. But the consolations arise from the virtuous work itself that we perform, and it seems that we have earned them through our own effort and are rightly consoled for having engaged in such deeds. But if we reflect upon this, we see that we experience the same joyful consolations in many of the things that can happen to us on earth; for example: when someone suddenly inherits a great fortune; when we suddenly see a person we love very much; when we succeed in a large and important business matter and of which everyone speaks well; when you see your husband or brother or son alive after someone has told you he is dead. I have seen the flow of tears from great consolations, and this has even happened to me at times. I think that just as these joyful consolations are natural so are those afforded us by the things of God, but these latter are of a nobler kind, although the others are not bad. In sum, joyful consolations in prayer have their beginning in our own human nature and end in God.

The spiritual delights begin in God, but human nature feels and enjoys them as much as it does those I mentioned—and much more. O Jesus, how I long to know how to explain this! For I discern, I think, a very recognizable difference, but I don't have the knowledge to be able to explain myself. May the Lord do so.

Now I remember a line that we say at Prime, in the latter part of the verse at the end of the last psalm: *Cum dilatasti cor meum* ["When you expand my heart" is a free translation. See Psalm 119:32.]. For anyone who has had much experience these words are sufficient to see the difference between consolations and spiritual delights; for anyone who has not, more words are needed. The consolations that were mentioned do not expand the heart; rather, they usually seem to constrain it a little—although there is the greatest consolation at seeing what is done for God. But some anxious tears come that in a way, it seems, are brought on by the passions.

My experience of this state (I mean of this joy and consolation that comes during meditation) is that if I began to weep over the Passion I didn't know how to stop until I got a severe headache; if I did so over my sins, the same thing happened. Our Lord granted me quite a favor. It is for these reasons sometimes that these tears flow and desires come, and they are furthered by human nature and one's temperament; but finally, as I have said, they end in God regardless of their nature. They are to be esteemed if there is the humility to understand that one is no better because of experiencing them, for it cannot be known whether they are all effects of love. When they are, the gift is God's.

For the most part, the souls in the previous dwelling places are the ones who have these devout feelings, for these souls work almost continually with the intellect, engaging in discursive thought and meditation. And they do well because nothing further has been given them; although they would be right if they engaged for a while in making acts of love, praising God, rejoicing in His goodness, that He is who He is, and in desiring His honor and glory. These acts should be made insofar as possible, for they are great awakeners of the will. Such souls would be well advised when the Lord gives them these acts not to abandon them for the sake of finishing the usual meditation.

I only wish to inform you that in order to profit by this path and ascend to the dwelling places we desire, the important thing is not to think much but to love much; and so do that which best stirs you to love. Perhaps we don't know what love is. I wouldn't be very surprised, because it doesn't consist in great delight but in desiring with strong determination to please God in everything, in striving, insofar as possible, not to offend Him, and in asking Him for the advancement of the honor and glory of His Son and the increase of the Catholic Church. These are the signs of love. Don't think the matter lies in thinking of nothing else and that if you become a little distracted all is lost.

I have been very afflicted at times in the midst of this turmoil of mind. For since the intellect is one of the soul's faculties, it was an arduous thing for me that it should be so restless at times. Ordinarily the mind flies about quickly, for only God can hold it fast in such a way as to make it seem that we are somehow loosed from this body. I have seen, I think, that the faculties of my soul were occupied and recollected in God while my mind on the other hand was distracted. This distraction puzzled me.

O Lord, take into account the many things we suffer on this path for lack of knowledge! The trouble is that since we do not think there is anything to know other than that we must think of You, we do not even know how to ask those who know nor do we understand what there is to ask. Terrible trials are suffered because we don't understand ourselves, and that which isn't bad at all but good we think is a serious fault. This lack of knowledge causes the afflictions of many people who engage in prayer; complaints about interior trials, at least to a great extent, by people who have no learning; melancholy and loss of health; and even the complete abandonment of prayer. For such persons don't reflect that there is an interior world here within us. Just as we cannot stop the movement of the heavens, but they proceed in rapid motion, so neither can we stop our mind; and then the faculties of the soul go with it, and we think we are lost and have wasted the time spent before God. But the soul is perhaps completely joined with Him in the dwelling places very close to the center while the mind is on the outskirts of the castle suffering from a thousand wild and poisonous beasts, and meriting by this suffering. As a result we should not be disturbed; nor should we abandon prayer, which is what the devil wants us to do. For the most part all the trials and disturbances come from our not understanding ourselves.

Spiritual Delights in Prayer

From *The Interior Castle, Fourth Dwelling Places,*
Chapter 2

Teresa contrasts consolations with the spiritual delights of the prayer of quiet. See the third "water" in the Life.

I have explained the nature of consolations in the spiritual life. Since they are sometimes mixed with our own passions, they are the occasion of loud sobbing; and I have heard some persons say they experience a tightening in the chest and even external bodily movements that they cannot restrain. But they must nonetheless be consoling, for, as I'm saying, the whole experience ends in the desire to please God and enjoy His Majesty's company.

The experiences that I call spiritual delight in God, that I termed elsewhere the prayer of quiet, are of a very different kind, as those of you who by the mercy of God have experienced them will know. Let's consider, for a better understanding, that we see two founts with two water troughs. (For I don't find anything more appropriate to explain some spiritual experiences than water.)

These two troughs are filled with water in different ways; with one the water comes from far away through many aqueducts and the use of much ingenuity; with the other the source of the water is right there, and the trough fills without any noise. If the spring is abundant, as is this one we are speaking about, the water overflows once the trough is filled, forming a large stream. There is no need of any skill, nor does the building of aqueducts have to continue; but water is always flowing from the spring.

The water coming from the aqueducts is comparable, in my opinion, to the consolations I mentioned that are drawn from meditation. For we obtain them through thoughts, assisting ourselves, using creatures to help our meditation, and tiring the intellect. Since, in the end, the consolation comes through our own efforts, noise is made when there has to be some replenishing of the benefits the consolation causes in the soul, as has been said.

With this other fount, the water comes from its own source which is God. And since His Majesty desires to do so—when He is pleased to grant some supernatural favor—He produces this delight with the greatest peace and quiet and sweetness in the very interior part of ourselves. I don't know from where or how, nor is that happiness and delight experienced, as are earthly consolations, in the heart. I mean there is no similarity at the beginning, for afterward the delight fills everything; this water overflows through all the dwelling places and faculties until reaching the body. That is why I said that it begins in God and ends in ourselves. For, certainly, as anyone who may have experienced it will see, the whole exterior man enjoys this spiritual delight and sweetness.

I was now thinking, while writing this, that the verse mentioned above, *dilatasti cor meum,* says the heart was expanded. I don't think the experience is something, as I say, that rises from the heart, but from another part still more interior, as from something deep. I think this must be the center of the soul, as I later came to understand and will mention at the end. For certainly I see secrets within ourselves that have often caused me to marvel. And how many more there must be! Oh, my Lord and my God, how great are Your grandeurs! We go about here below like foolish little shepherds, for while it seems that we are getting some knowledge of You it must amount to no more than nothing; for even in our own selves there are great secrets that we don't understand.

To return to the verse, what I think is helpful in it for explaining this matter is the idea of expansion. It seems that since that heavenly water begins to rise from this spring I'm mentioning that is deep within us, it swells and expands our whole interior being, producing ineffable blessings; nor does the soul even understand what is given to it there. It perceives a fragrance, let us say for now, as though there were in that interior depth a brazier giving off sweet-smelling perfumes.

No light is seen, nor is the place seen where the brazier is; but the warmth and the fragrant fumes spread through the entire soul and even often enough, as I have said, the body shares in them. See now that you understand me; no heat is felt, nor is there the scent of any perfume, for the experience is more delicate than an experience of these things; but I use the examples only so as to explain it to you. This spiritual delight is not something that can be imagined, because however diligent our efforts we cannot acquire it. The very experience of it makes us realize that it is not of the same metal as we ourselves but fashioned from the purest gold of the divine wisdom. Here, in my opinion, the faculties are not united but absorbed and looking as though in wonder at what they see.

Recollection and the Prayer of Quiet

From *The Interior Castle, Fourth Dwelling Places,*
Chapter 3

*Teresa backtracks to write about recollection as the transition
from meditation to the prayer of quiet. This corresponds to the
second "water" of the* Life.

I want to mention another kind of prayer. It is a recollection
that also seems to me to be supernatural because it doesn't
involve being in the dark or closing the eyes, nor does it consist
in any exterior thing, since without first wanting to do so, one
does close one's eyes and desire solitude. It seems that without
any contrivance the edifice is being built, by means of this
recollection, for the prayer that was mentioned. The senses and
exterior things seem to be losing their hold because the soul is
recovering what it had lost.

They say that the soul enters within itself and, at other
times, that it rises above itself. With such terminology I
wouldn't know how to clarify anything. Let us suppose that
these senses and faculties (for I have already mentioned that
these powers are the people of this castle, which is the image

I have taken for my explanation) have gone outside and have walked for days and years with strangers—enemies of the well-being of the castle. Having seen their perdition they have already begun to approach the castle even though they may not manage to remain inside because the habit of doing so is difficult to acquire. But still they are not traitors, and they walk in the environs of the castle. Once the great King, who is in the center dwelling place of this castle, sees their good will, He desires in His wonderful mercy to bring them back to Him. Like a good shepherd, with a whistle so gentle that even they themselves almost fail to hear it, He makes them recognize His voice and stops them from going so far astray so that they will return to their dwelling place. And this shepherd's whistle has such power that they abandon the exterior things in which they were estranged from Him and enter the castle.

I don't think I've ever explained it as clearly as I have now. When God grants the favor it is a great help to seek Him within where He is found more easily and in a way more beneficial to us than when sought in creatures, as Saint Augustine says after having looked for Him in many places. Don't think this recollection is acquired by the intellect striving to think about God within itself, or by the imagination imagining Him within itself. Such efforts are good and an excellent kind of meditation because they are founded on a truth, which is that God is within us. But this isn't the prayer of recollection because it is something each one can do—with the help of God, as should be understood of everything. But what I'm speaking of comes in a different way. Sometimes before one begins to think of God, these people are already inside the castle. I don't know in what way or how they heard their shepherd's whistle. It wasn't through the ears, because nothing is heard. But one noticeably senses a gentle drawing inward. It seems to me I have read where it was compared to a hedgehog curling up or a turtle drawing into its shell. (The one who wrote this example must have understood the experience well.) But these creatures draw inward whenever they want. In the case of this recollection, it doesn't come when we want it but when God wants to grant us the favor. I for myself hold that when His Majesty grants it, He does so to persons who are already beginning to despise the things of the world. So I believe that if we desire to make room for His Majesty, He will give not only this but more, and give it to those whom He begins to call to advance further.

But as I said elsewhere the reason why in this kind of prayer—that is, the kind that is like the flowing spring in which the water does not come through aqueducts—the soul restrains itself or is restrained is its realization that it doesn't understand what it desires; and so the mind wanders from one extreme to the other, like a fool unable to rest in anything. (I am referring to the kind of prayer this dwelling place began with, for I have joined the prayer of recollection, which I should have mentioned first, with this one. The prayer of recollection is much less intense than the prayer of spiritual delight from God that I mentioned. But it is the beginning through which one goes to the other; for in the prayer of recollection, meditation, or the work of the intellect, must not be set aside.) The will has such deep rest in its God that the clamor of the intellect is a terrible bother to it. There is no need to pay any attention to this clamor, for doing so would make the will lose much of what it enjoys. But one should leave the intellect go and surrender oneself into the arms of love, for His Majesty will teach the soul what it must do at that point. Almost everything lies in finding oneself unworthy of so great a good and in being occupied with giving thanks.

The Soul as a Silkworm

From *The Interior Castle, Fifth Dwelling Places,* Chapter 2

In discussing the prayer of union, Teresa uses the image of the life cycle of a silkworm as another way of describing the spiritual life.

With regard to the nature of union, I don't believe I'd know how to say anything more. To explain things better I want to use a helpful comparison; it is good for making us see how, even though we can do nothing in this work done by the Lord, we can do much by disposing ourselves so that His Majesty may grant us this favor.

You must have already heard about His marvels manifested in the way silk originates, for only He could have invented something like that. The silkworms come from seeds about the size of little grains of pepper. (I have never seen this but heard of it, and so if something in the explanation gets distorted it won't be my fault.) When the warm weather comes and the leaves begin to appear on the mulberry tree, the seeds start to live, for they are dead until then. The worms nourish themselves on mulberry leaves until, having grown to full size, they settle on some twigs. There with their little mouths they themselves go about spinning the silk and making some very thick little cocoons in which they enclose themselves. The silkworm, which is fat and ugly, then dies, and a little white butterfly which is very pretty, comes forth from the cocoon.

This silkworm, then, starts to live when by the heat of the Holy Spirit it begins to benefit through the general help given to us all by God and through the remedies left by Him to His Church, by going to confession, reading good books, and hearing sermons, which are the remedies that a soul, dead in its carelessness and sins and placed in the midst of occasions, can make use of. It then begins to live and to sustain itself by these things, and by good meditations, until it is grown. Its being grown is what is relevant to what I'm saying, for these other things have little importance here.

Well, once this silkworm is grown it begins to spin the silk and build the house wherein it will die. I would like to point out here that this house is Christ. Somewhere, it seems to me, I have read or heard that our life is hidden in Christ or in God (both are the same), or that our life is Christ. His Majesty Himself, as He does in this prayer of union, becomes the dwelling place we build for ourselves. Not that we can take God away or build Him up, but we can take away from ourselves and build up, as do these little silkworms. For we will not have finished doing all that we can in this work when, to the little we do, which is nothing, God will unite Himself, with His greatness, and give it such high value that the Lord Himself will become the reward of this work.

Therefore, courage, my daughters! Let's be quick to do this work and weave this little cocoon by getting rid of our self-love and self-will, our attachment to any earthly thing, and by performing deeds of penance, prayer, mortification, obedience, and of all the other things you know. Let it die; let this silkworm die, as it does in completing what it was created to do! And you will see how we see God, as well as ourselves placed inside His greatness, as is this little silkworm within its cocoon.

Now, then, let's see what this silkworm does, for that's the reason I've said everything else. When the soul is, in this prayer, truly dead to the world, a little white butterfly comes forth. Oh, greatness of God! How transformed the soul is when it comes out of this prayer after having been placed within the greatness of God and so closely joined with Him for a little while—in my opinion the union never lasts for as much as a half hour. Truly, I tell you that the soul doesn't recognize itself. Look at the difference there is between an ugly worm and a little white butterfly; that's what the difference is here. The soul doesn't know how it could have merited so much good—from where this good may have come I mean, for it well knows that it doesn't merit this blessing. It sees within itself a desire to praise the Lord; it would want to dissolve and die a thousand deaths for Him. It soon begins to experience a desire to suffer great trials without its being able to do otherwise. There are the strongest desires for penance, for solitude, and that all might know God; and great pain comes to it when it sees that He is offended.

Oh, now, to see the restlessness of this little butterfly, even though it has never been quieter and calmer in its life, is something to praise God for! And the difficulty is that it doesn't know where to alight and rest. Since it has experienced such wonderful rest, all that it sees on earth displeases it, especially if God gives it this wine often. Almost each time it gains new treasures. It no longer has any esteem for the works it did while a worm, which was to weave the cocoon little by little; it now has wings. How can it be happy walking step by step when it can fly? On account of its desires, everything it can do for God becomes little in its own eyes. The weakness it previously seemed to have with regard to doing penance it now finds is its strength. Its attachment to relatives or friends or wealth is now so looked upon that it grieves when obliged to do what is necessary in this regard so as not to offend God. Everything wearies it, for it has learned through experience that creatures cannot give it true rest.

Appendix

Reading Spiritual Classics for Personal and Group Formation

Many Christians today are searching for more spiritual depth, for something more than simply being good church members. That quest may send them to the spiritual practices of New Age movements or of Eastern religions such as Zen Buddhism. Christians, though, have their own long spiritual tradition, a tradition rich with wisdom, variety, and depth.

The great spiritual classics testify to that depth. They do not concern themselves with mystical flights for a spiritual elite. Rather, they contain very practical advice and insights that can support and shape the spiritual growth of any Christian. We can all benefit by sitting at the feet of the masters (both male and female) of Christian spirituality.

Reading spiritual classics is different from most of the reading we do. We have learned to read to master a text and extract information from it. We tend to read quickly, to get through a text. And we summarize as we read, seeking the main point. In reading spiritual classics, though, we allow the text to master and form us. Such formative reading goes more slowly, more reflectively, allowing time for God to speak to us through the text. God's word for us may come as easily from a minor point or even an aside as from the major point.

Formative reading requires that you approach the text in humility. Read as a seeker, not as an expert. Don't demand that the text meet your expectations for what an "enlightened" author should write. Humility means accepting the author as another imperfect human, a product of his or her own time and situation. Learn to celebrate what is foundational in an author's writing without being overly disturbed by what is peculiar to the author's life and times. Trust the text as a gift from both God and the author, offered to you for your benefit—to help you grow in Christ.

To read formatively, you must also slow down. Feel free to reread a passage that seems to speak specially to you. Stop from time to time to reflect on what you have been reading. Keep a journal for these reflections. Often the act of writing can itself prompt further, deeper reflection. Keep your notebook open and your pencil in hand as you read. You might not get back to that wonderful insight later. Don't worry that you are not getting through an entire passage—or even the first paragraph! Formative reading is about depth rather than breadth, quality rather than quantity. As you read, seek God's direction for your own life. Timeless truths have their place but may not be what is most important for your own formation here and now.

As you read the passage, you might keep some of these questions running through your mind:

- How is what I'm reading true of my own life? Where does it reflect my own *experience!*
- How does this text challenge me? What new *direction* does it offer me?
- What must I change to put what I am reading into practice? How can I *incarnate* it, let this word become flesh in my life?

You might also devote special attention to sections that upset you. What is the source of the disturbance? Do you want to argue theology? Are you turned off by cultural differences? Or have you been skewered by an insight that would turn your life upside down if you took it seriously? Let your journal be a dialogue with the text.

If you find yourself moving from reading the text to chewing over its implications to praying, that's great! Spiritual reading is really the first step in an ancient way of prayer called *lectio divina* or "divine reading." Reading leads naturally into reflection on what you have read (meditation). As you reflect on what the text might mean for your life, you may well want to ask for God's help in living out any new insights or direction you have perceived (prayer). Sometimes such prayer may lead you further into silently abiding in God's presence (contemplation). And, of course, the process is only really completed when it begins to make a difference in the way we live (incarnation).

As good as it is to read spiritual classics in solitude, it is even better to join with others in a small group for mutual formation or "spiritual direction in common." This is *not* the same as a study group that talks *about* spiritual classics. A group for mutual formation would have similar goals as for an individual's reading: to allow the text to shine its light on the *experiences* of the group members, to suggest new *directions* for their lives and practical ways of *incarnating* these directions. Such a group might agree to focus on one short passage from a classic at each meeting (even if members have read more). Discussion usually goes much deeper if all the members have already read and reflected on the passage before the meeting and bring their journals.

Such groups need to watch for several potential problems. It is easy to go off on a tangent (especially if it takes the focus off the members' own experience and onto generalities). At such times a group leader might bring the group's attention back to the text: "What does our author say about that?" Or, "How do we experience that in our own lives?" When a group member shares a problem, others may be tempted to try to "fix" it. This is much less helpful than sharing similar experiences and how they were handled (for good or ill). "Sharing" someone else's problems (whether that person is in or out of the group) should be strongly discouraged.

One person could be designated as leader, to be responsible for opening and closing prayers; to be the first to share or respond to the text; and to keep notes during the discussion to highlight recurring themes, challenges, directives, or practical steps. These responsibilities could also be shared among several members of the group or rotated.

For further information about formative reading of spiritual classics, try *A Practical Guide to Spiritual Reading* by Susan Annette Muto. *Shaped by the Word: The Power of Scripture in Spiritual Formation* by M. Robert Mulholland Jr. covers formative reading of the Bible. *Good Things Happen: Experiencing Community in Small Groups* by Dick Westley is an excellent resource on forming small groups of all kinds.